HOW TO SUCCEED IN COLLEGE WHILE STILL HAVING A TERRIFIC SOCIAL LIFE

WANT BETTER GRADES AND HAPPINESS IN YOUR LIFE? WANT TO ELIMINATE, STRESS AND ANXIETY?

RUSSEL JACOBS

BOOK DESCRIPTION

EVERYONE KNOWS THAT THE EARLY BIRD CATCHES THE WORM—BUT NOT EVERYONE KNOWS HOW IT'S DONE.

Studies have shown that early risers earn more money. They're happier and more productive, and perhaps surprisingly, they often report feeling better rested than those who get up late.

Waking up early exposes you to more daylight, which in turn increases the levels of serotonin released by the brain—and that means an elevated mood, a calmer outlook, and increased focus. When you think of it that way, it's clear to see why waking up early would make you more productive.

As a college student, you're at the **perfect time in your life** to adopt the habit of rising early. Any good habit you form now will be one you maintain for your entire life. And with your career still ahead of you, the success you can achieve by adopting this habit *now* is incredible.

The idea of waking up early daunts most young people, and it's true that if you throw yourself into it without a clear strategy, you might find it difficult.

But when you go in with a plan, you'll find it's **easier than you think**, and you'll start reaping the rewards immediately.

You'll see your energy levels improve, your grades get better, and your mood stabilizes. It's the most straightforward life hack there is.

In *How to Succeed In College While Still Having a Terrific Social Life*, you'll be given a precise roadmap for becoming **not just a morning person, but an enthusiastic one**. You'll discover:

- A **clear strategy** for getting the most out of early rising, even if you think you're not a morning person.
- Four key reasons why 5 am is the best time for you to start your day

- The #1 reason that stops people from getting up early, and how you can guarantee avoiding the same mistake
- **Solid techniques for retraining your body** for a new sleep cycle
- The reason why rising with the sun helped *Twitter CEO Jack Dorsey* become a billionaire and one of the most successful players in the tech industry
- How 'VAT' is going to change your life (no, not *that* kind of VAT)
- Why goal setting is essential, and exactly how you can do it efficiently
- How to design a bespoke morning routine that fits you perfectly
- The secret to being able to **fall asleep in 120 seconds or less**
- The biggest psychological roadblock preventing you from achieving your goals, yet how you can plow through it

And much more.

If you're anything like most college students, the idea of getting up early is probably filling you with dread. That's normal, but here's a secret—that feeling doesn't last long.

Once you've trained yourself in the art of early rising and have felt its power, **you'll never look back**.

How to Succeed In College While Still Having a Terrific Social Life, offers you the precise formula for a purpose-driven life full of success and achievement.

Be the early bird: learn how to get ahead and catch that worm.

If you want to set yourself up for a lifetime of happiness and success, scroll up and click "Add to Cart" right now. It's time to stop hitting 'snooze'.

CONTENTS

INTRODUCTION

Greetings, sleepy heads! I'm glad you're here. I've written this book for people just like you – people for whom tapping the snooze bar has been elevated to the level of a sacred morning ritual.

"Five more minutes!" is your rallying cry.

Don't feel too bad. It was once mine, as well. I was where you are now—living the student life.

Frankly, people don't give college students enough credit. You've left home—or are about to leave home—for college/university. You are entering the academic world with all its demands.

You may have a part-time job to help sustain yourself financially, and you most definitely have a social life.

You're reading because you're locked in mortal combat with the early hours of the morning.

That also was me once.

Today, I'm a father of 3 and a successful part-time entrepreneur. But once upon a time, I was the guy who was always late for class, tired and cranky from keeping late nights socializing. Oh yes, I loved to party.

But the thing is, my ability to focus in class, do assignments, and keep myself together in general, was horrible. My nocturnal habits might have caused that. Or maybe it was just part of being young. I was no fan of early mornings back then, but I am now, and I'm going to tell you in this book why that shift happened.

I'm going to tell you here about the tremendous changes that occurred in my life due to rising at 5 am, six days a week. I'd always been a night owl, and changing my habits transformed my life and its quality.

I've shared this precise road map of becoming an enthusiastic, shiny morning person with friends, relatives, and colleagues. People couldn't believe the stunning change in me and wanted to know how I did it, so I wrote this book to share some essential life hacks with the people around me.

And now my friend, I'm going to share them with you. As you read, you'll discover how rising at 5 am won't just improve your grades but will make you a happier and more productive person—for life.

I wish I'd known all this when I started college life. I passionately believe the stress, anxiety, and occasional depression I experienced would have been averted. My purpose here is to make sure you do not repeat my mistakes. I am equipping you with crucial knowledge as you embark on adulthood.

Starting early with good habits is the best way to make them stick and to form the solid foundation required for success.

Read on. Find out how you can revolutionize your life with simple disciplines and become the early bird who gets the fattest worm every time.

1

SETTING THE STAGE

Y ou're reading this because you're ready for a change, aren't you? Of course, you are! You want better grades. You want to feel less anxious, reduce college life stress, and eliminate your depressive episodes. You want to face each day feeling psychologically and physically prepared. We have all been there. Maybe to you, getting up at 5 am seems antithetical to those goals.

But nothing could be further from the truth.

As I said earlier, I used to have a difficult time rising early myself. I was that college kid whose dorm room told a story of late nights and chronic disorganization. Empty ramen noodle cups were my décor scheme, and they allowed me to "cram" when I procrastinated studying for exams or writing papers and not have to take time for a nutritious meal.

But the Ramen thing was really about laziness. At that age, I couldn't be bothered to feed myself properly. It was easier to grab the noodle cup and feed my body with carbs, fats, salt, and chemicals.

Eating those notoriously nutrition-challenged noodle cups was only an emblem of a much bigger problem. I had convinced myself that it was my core personality and not just a bad habit. The reality is, I was just a hapless college student, far from mom and her casseroles and BLTs. Ramen was a college tradition, and heck, I wanted to be part of that!

Why not?

My insistence that I was beyond redemption absolved me of all responsibility for my failure to change my perspective on life. But guess what? I later changed, and so can you.

Here's the thing: there is this myth 5 am is an "ungodly" hour of the day. I know that because I used to cling to myths like this to justify my chaotic life in the dorm. Let's start setting the stage by dispelling this and other myths around the subject of early rising.

AN UNGODLY HOUR

I used to believe that 5 am was an ungodly hour. It was an article of faith for me as a night owl. But those days are gone.

There is nothing ungodly about the hour. Five am as good a time as any to start your day, but when you're focused on achievement, it's the best time of all, and here's why:

- **Better organization** – You will have time at your disposal to organize your calendar. If you plan your meals, you will have time to do it well. Being organized is one of the critical pillars of success.
- **Exercise** – With more time at your disposal, you'll have fewer excuses not to exercise regularly. Even if all you're down for is walking the dog, you'll have time for it.
- **Tranquility** – The early morning hours, before the rest of the world has awakened, are a peaceful time allowing for quiet reflection, catching up on current events, or doing a Yoga routine!
- **Taking control of your internal clock** – Choosing 5 am as your set time to rise will also prime your body into a new sleep pattern.

You'll find that you go to bed earlier because you get up earlier.

As you can see, 5 am looks a lot different when you think about what you can do with the time. And no, after a long day of classes, you're not going to accomplish much at night. The early morning is the ideal time to take hold of the loose threads of your life. You're fresh, rested, and alert.

I CAN'T DO IT! IT'S THE WAY I'M WIRED!

Let's be honest. The statement in the subtitle above is an excuse.

Rising at 5 am has absolutely nothing to do with you as a person. There is almost no reason that anyone who sincerely desires to make this change can't.

The truth is that once we've reached adulthood, 8 hours of sleep should be enough for most people. We were all teenagers once. But as adults, we don't need as much sleep as we once did.

According to the National Sleep Foundation, adults require between 7 and 9 hours per night. Teenagers, between 8 and 10 hours.

The hour you rise has nothing to do with the way you're "wired." It's much more about what you're accustomed to. You're accustomed to rising at 7:30 am and giving yourself 20 minutes to shoot out the door. That doesn't mean you're wired that way. It just means you've set up your life for late nights and later mornings.

WON'T I BE TIRED?

Of course, you'll be tired—if you don't hit the sack earlier! This is a lifestyle change that you're contemplating for academic performance and your future success in adult life, so it's worth it!

And you even get to wake up as late as you like, one day a week![1]

So, sure. You're going to lose some of your late-night hours. But isn't that when you're tired? Because you get up late, you defer required actions like studying and exercising to later in the day. You either end up doing them when you really should be resting to prepare for the new day or not doing them at all. When you get up early and have a plan for those early morning hours ready to go, your goals are met, with no excuses. You have re-jigged your lifestyle to make everything possible.

Next, let's examine why rising at 5 am is an excellent idea because it carries tremendous benefits for your health, wellness, and success.

SCIENCE SAYS, "GET UP EARLY!"

I think it's fair to say that almost everyone reading has, at some point, experienced the early morning.

Maybe it was a road trip to Disneyland as a kid, or maybe you stayed up all night and witnessed the rare spectacle of the dawn coming up like thunder.

You may have experienced this time of day. So, what about the early morning struck you most?

What I've noticed about my early mornings is that I'm usually the first person in our neighborhood to wake up. I look out the kitchen window, and not one other light is on at 5 am. The quiet, when traffic hasn't started rumbling pass, and the only sound you hear is birds chirping, can be a relating and quiet time.

As 21st Century people, how often do we get to experience that kind of tranquility in our busy lives?

Well, you can experience it six days a week if you get up at 5 am to enjoy it!

And this pleasant time of day, spent in blessed peace, can do amazing things for you. The absence of noise and the sense that the world is still sleeping is highly beneficial to your health.

Don't believe me? Check this out:

- Oxygen levels in the brain increase.
- Blood pressure reduces.
- Migraines reduce (for those who suffer from them).
- Mental health improves.

In 2008, the Journal of General Psychology released a study that revealed that those who rose early enjoyed increased productivity. Part of that effect is linked to the focus and discipline that flow from sticking to a sleeping/waking routine.

The next day starts at night. This statement is affirmed by another study published in the Cognitive Therapy and Research Journal. Those who stay up late at night, then rise early the next day are at risk of developing depression. The key to optimizing the benefits of rising early is establishing a set time to sleep and wake up.

This habit helps you establish a sleep cycle that isn't plagued by negative thoughts that keep so many people from falling asleep and staying asleep. Negative thoughts are significantly minimized because you get things done by getting up early, and when the end of the day comes – your brain and body are ready to sleep! If you cannot turn off negative thoughts, and it's proving to be persistent, my advice is that you seek medical attention from a competent Psychiatrist of your choice.

YOU'RE UP AT 5 AM — NOW WHAT?

So, you've set your alarm, and now, you're awake at 5 am! What do you do?

Well, that's up to you! What you do with this time is your decision. I will talk about structuring this newly found morning time to work for you in the next chapter. For now, the general framework goes like this:

- When you get up at 5 am, you're giving yourself two full hours to accomplish some goals. How will you do that? You will make those two hours count by setting them aside for a precise morning routine, which you will accomplish before leaving for your first class.
- If that class starts at 8 am, you have a three-hour window, so factor in preparation and transit time. And remember, you need 7-9 hours of sleep each night, so if you're getting up

at 5 am, get to bed in time to sleeps the hours you need.

ELIMINATE THE PROBLEM

Most communities I know and hear of are noisy. Some people are blessed to live in quieter enclaves, but those are hard to find, especially in college communities.

If you're concerned about noise preventing you from falling asleep, there are several things you can do to solve the issue.

You may live in a noisy residential hall or a shared apartment, so noise will be a factor. Noise-reducing earplugs are one way to limit ambient noise's ability to prevent or interrupt sleep. But don't rule out white noise machines or playing soothing sounds to kill the nocturnal racket that keeps you tossing and turning instead of sleeping.

Another impediment to people falling asleep these days is the omnipresence of artificial light.

Streetlights, security lights, your neighbors' porch lights, TVs, and smartphones—these can all disrupt your brain's production of melatonin, the "sleep hormone". So lengthy exposure to the light, especially 2 hours before bedtime, can keep you awake.

As you probably know, melatonin is available in supplement form, but producing your own is a much better way to enjoy the calming effects this natural substance, produced by the human body, is known for. It's the body's natural sleep aid—made to order, so give it the help it needs to do its thing.

But all you need to correct that problem is a blackout curtain or a lining for your existing curtains. These cut excess light and, if appropriately fitted, make your sleeping area a dark, cozy cave.

So, keep screens out of the bedroom.

In a dorm room, this may be a challenge.

But if you have a TV in the room, it should be off for 2 hours before you sleep.

Similarly, mobile devices, tablets, and laptops should not be in use 2 hours before you go to sleep for most people. Here's why – electronic devices emit "blue light." According to a study done by the National Sleep Foundation, this type of light emits a shorter wavelength, suppressing melatonin production in the body.

Melatonin is a hormone governing the sleep/wake cycle. When night falls, melatonin production kicks into high gear. By the crack of dawn, the presence of melatonin in the blood is almost undetectable.

Now that we've set the stage, we're ready to start talking about the "big stuff," like what you believe your purpose in life is. While the question may seem overwhelming, you probably already have an idea of what that it is. The purpose of this book is to define it and to leverage your early-rising lifestyle to get you there. Without knowing what your purpose is, this project might have already failed before even getting started.

A big part of that is setting the morning routine we were talking about. Plotting quiet morning time is a learned behavior, and no one is born knowing how to do this. Everyone needs to learn to take their destiny into their own hands by effectively using the time they have.

So, let's move on to being reborn as a morning person—the reason you are reading this. Get ready because you are about to discover a whole new way of using those precious morning hours productively and intelligently!

[1] If you suffer from sleep-related problems as a medical condition, keep the same sleep schedule, even on weekends.

2

PURPOSE. GOALS. MORNING ROUTINE

"Accept no one's definition of your life; define yourself."

— HARVEY FIERSTEIN

L ife is a one-time offer. You don't get a "do-over." That's why I'm so passionate about sharing the advice in this book with you. You're young—just starting out. You have decades stretched out before you to learn, achieve, and succeed.

With the advice I'm offering you here, you'll be well-positioned to make your life exactly what you want it to be.

You will have a running start on everyone who has convinced themselves that they're just not morning people.

You may not be a morning person right this minute, as you read. But by the time you turn the last page of this book over, you'll be that early bird who gets the fattest worm—or whatever it is you're pursuing. Your degree, success, and life you desire are all within reach when you take the bull by the horns and get off the blocks early in the morning while everyone else is still sleeping.

But everything starts with your purpose. Who are you?

What are you here to do? How do you intend to achieve it? What are the benchmarks along the way that indicate you're moving toward that purpose? Once you have clarity on the answers to these questions from the get-go, you will handle most of the challenges you face without many difficulties. These challenges may even be entirely avoided because of the choices and decisions you will make due to being clear on your purpose.

These are big questions. I get it. But creating a vision of what you're here to do is the fire lit in the belly. It's in your knowledge of your life's trajectory from which real power is derived. Your purpose is what will fuel your way forward and propel you out of bed like a heat-seeking missile!

ASKING THE RIGHT QUESTIONS

I was young once, as I've explained.

I believed that my life goals would magically materialize at some point and that all would be revealed.

But plotting out your life's course isn't a matter of waiting for it to come to you. Like Harvey Fierstein said in the earlier quote, you define yourself.

You plot your life. That doesn't come from outside you. It comes from your dreams and aptitudes and how you're forming those into a vocation at college.

So, here are some key questions to ask on the way to defining your life's purpose:

- Am I at the right university or college for what I want to become?
- Is my choice of major right?
- Are my friends the right friends to support me as I move forward?

You must have probably heard the phrase, "you are the average of the five people you spend your time with". It's true based on my experience.

- Are my extra-curricular activities supporting my life's purpose?

But there are many other probing questions you need to ask yourself right now to make your new morning routine effective. With a clear definition of purpose, you light the fire in your belly that pushes you toward it. So, let's take a deep dive into finding your purpose and how to go about it.

WHAT DO I GET LOST IN?

What we love, we want to do all the time. For some, that's cycling. For others, embroidery or another crafting pursuit. Some get lost in current affairs, or philosophical questions, or even math. What you get lost in is what you love. It's what makes you lose track of time because you're so engaged in what you're doing. It's all there is.

So, ask yourself: What do I love? Will the major you've chosen involve that love? Is the university or college you're attending developing the skills and knowledge base required? Whatever it is you love, probably comes effortlessly to you. It's usually the case that people become attracted to those things they have specific gifts for accomplishing.

That doesn't mean you don't need to perfect your passion. Everyone does! Even Yehudi Menuhin had to practice his violin for countless hours to become the giant he was in classical music. Even Hank Aaron struck out. We all need to learn our craft.

But when you pursue that one thing that gets you so focused, you can't tear yourself away: you're forming your future.

It comes easily for a reason—because it's probably the path you should be taking.

STATING YOUR LIFE'S PURPOSE

When do you feel most comfortable and "right" in your world? Maybe it's when you're embroiled in a research project or writing a paper. Or maybe it's when you're bringing others together to accomplish something.

When plugged into whatever you get lost in, what you love, and what comes easily to you, the comfort level you experience when these three factors align is a strong indication that you're on the right path.

But your heart is the ultimate determinant. You know what your truth is. You know what you love doing, what you're good at, and who you are. Running all the factors involved through your heart reveals how authentic you are with yourself. If you can't be authentic now, when are you going to be? You're too young to have reached a state of brittle inauthenticity. Now is the time to allow your youthful honesty out to play. It will help you state your life's purpose with confidence and integrity.

Because if your heart is not in it, you and I both know what that means, don't we?

YOUR PURPOSE IS A BUILDING PROJECT

Some people say you need to find your purpose.

But it's not "out there." It's all in you. You need to find the pieces that amount to your purpose, put them together, and build on them.

It will not "come." But it will materialize from the font of your self-knowledge and your purpose's continual call to you. The pieces will fall together.

And yes, I said, "pieces." Purpose isn't a one-trick pony. Purpose is where you find your calling, and that's not one-dimensional, by any means.

Your purpose is determined by the influences which have captured your fascination and interest.

Is a Biology degree compatible with interning for Doctors Without Borders? Is an Arts degree at odds with interest in sustainable agriculture to feed the world? By no means! People are not one-dimensional, and our passions take us to places we never believed we might go.

Build your life's purpose by choosing those pieces that fit together and form the public template for who you are and propel you forward and nurture you as you go.

And at some point, wonder of wonders, your purpose may change. One day, you find yourself committed to what you believe is your primary purpose, only to see an opportunity that transforms that purpose into something even more spectacular the next day. Nothing is written in stone, and nothing is forever.

Life is dynamic, and so is your purpose. It's about your place within a greater purpose. What you bring to that great purpose is your sense of mission, and that may have multiple applications that haven't yet occurred to you.

These days, people may have many careers in one life-time. Your degree may have applications that will only become clear 20 years from now. You may feel called to take what you've learned in a new direction—or to a new way of doing things. Again—nothing is written in stone, and what you're building is something completely new.

Isn't that a beautiful thought? But it's true. Your purpose is unique, flexible, and mutable. Within a framework that serves an overarching purpose, you may take your gifts, passion, and love in any direction. But it's the framework that defines what you've been put here to do.

FEELING YOUR PURPOSE

This data-driven society seems to do everything according to benchmarks and measurable results.

But you can't measure instinct.

Instinct is that part of you that continues to live in the pre-verbal world. It's the gnawing in the pit of your stomach, the hair rising on the back of your arms. It's the mysterious feeling that where you are is where you're supposed to be.

And your instincts will let you know if you're wandering off the path you've set for yourself. It will tell you some exciting things that you should take note of and heed. It's your instincts that tell you when something's wrong.

Your human brain then takes up the question, connecting instinct to reason, to work out the rationality of the message your instincts are sending you.

Let's examine what you might learn from your instincts while moving toward understanding your life's purpose.

You can't wait to get back to what you were doing yesterday before you went to sleep.

Your instincts may tell you something that may seem counterintuitive when you're working twice as hard because of that fire in your belly I was talking about earlier. They'll tell you you're not tired. That you're moving toward something worth having, so you not only don't want to put it aside, you simply can't!

You're accomplishing what you need to, effortlessly.

Self-doubt is human. We all suffer from it at some point. But when you're on the right trajectory, all will seem to fall into place, and you'll feel that your progress is effortless. You do not doubt in your mind that you're where you're supposed to be. And all that human self-doubt is silenced.

That Law of Attraction thingy kicks in.

Are you noticing that you're attracting people with a purpose that's not unlike your own? Well, whether you believe it or not, or whether there's scientific evidence or not, this is what happens when you're on the right track.

You are attracting the actors needed to continue moving forward. Don't question it. The people you're attracting are there for the same reason you are, and they're part of your story.

Money no longer rules you.

Finding your purpose means you're willing to do what it takes to realize it. Take a pay cut? Sure! You don't care. That liberation you feel as you become fearless in the pursuit of your purpose applies to the bondage of a regular paycheck, as well. You're going after something better, so money *no longer shackles you to work you're not interested in doing, a car, or a house, etc. You know you'll triumph because your instincts are telling you as much.

When you find your purpose, your sense of peace is enormous. You're content with what you're doing, and you're also confident that you are created to do this.

The fear that rules far too many people is dispelled when you know you're moving in the direction you're destined to move in. All the anxiety you once struggled with melts away. The money will come, and the people will come. You're on your way, and you're excited and endlessly happy about it.

But whether you know your life's purpose yet or not, getting to where you want to be to fulfill it is a matter of setting goals and then achieving them.

SETTING GOALS GETS YOU THERE

So, now that you're either validating or figuring out your purpose, you're reading to grab hold of the goals that can get you there.

You know the "why?" Now, it's time to unravel the "how?"

Setting goals is dynamic benchmarking, driven by your purpose. In setting goals, you're taking steps. Realizing your goals, therefore, involves taking incremental steps toward realizing and living out your purpose.

Goals allow you to deconstruct your purpose as a series of actions. Further, they give cause for celebration. Every goal realized is a step closer to living in and for your purpose.

SO, HOW DO YOU SET YOUR GOALS?

Setting goals is all about defining them. Many people don't think about goal setting, as they don't know what they want.

But if you're here, it's clear you do.

So, let's find out about a simple acronym that spells "defined goals": SMART.

Here's what it stands for:

- **SPECIFIC** – "Work harder" is not a goal. "Complete Project X by (insert date) is a goal.
- **MEASURABLE** – Achieving a goal means it's done. Each step you take to achieve it is a step toward completion, so check the steps off. Only when all the steps have been taken is your goal wholly achieved.
- **ACHIEVABLE**- Be realistic. "Pie in the sky" is visioning or dreaming, and that's ok, but it's not goal setting.

Choose goals you have the time and resources to complete, which are concrete and within reach.

- **RELEVANT** – Goals achieved toward your purpose are valid because they're relevant to that purpose. Getting your dog's toenails clipped is not a goal for that reason. You feel rewarded by achieving the goals that are steppingstones toward your purpose.

- **TIMED** – Set yourself deadlines to reach your goals. A goal without a timeline is just an idea. When your goals aren't time bound, they're too easy to let slip away.

DEVELOPING YOURSELF WITH GOALS

You only have so many hours in the day. That's true, even if you're adding more productive hours by rising at 5 am!

Your personal development is a large part of realizing your purpose. Along the way, you'll take notes about various skills you know would make a difference to your journey toward that purpose.

As you identify these skills, you will need to prioritize which is most relevant and pressing to develop and in which order.

Rate the personal development goals you've identified from 1 to 10, with 1 as your most important goal on the list.

Then, see how they all fit together. Let's take, for example, that one of your personal development goals is to travel to Paris and have a fantastic experience, another is to widen your circle of connections in France in your area of interest, and the next is to be fluent in French. Here is what I'd do to realize all 3 of them:

- Take a French-language conversation class.
- Get involved in circles where your French-speaking peers meet. This could be achieved by joining meetups that organize both off-line (Paris) and online meetings. You will start creating meaningful connections here.
- After taking care of the first two steps, I can almost guarantee your trip to France will be worth it as you will have more than a fantastic experience.

And as you set your goals, avoid falling into the logic vs. emotion trap. Logic and emotion should fit together seamlessly when you're discussing something as personal as goals. You've called on your instincts and feelings to guide you, but you need reason—the seat of logic—to guide you toward the best course of action. Reason works with instinct, so it follows that logic and emotion also inform each other. Don't exclude your feelings, even if you fear you may not be leaning as hard on logic as you might typically be. How you feel about something is usually the truth—or, at least, your truth.

HAVE A PLAN

The first thing you'll need is a tool to plot out the realization of your goals. You can use a paper calendar for this or a notebook, but many online tools may also be used. I'll recommend Google Calendar here, as that's the tool I use.

Plot your course by biting off only what you can chew. Over-programing yourself is the road to self-sacrifice, so set a realistic schedule—remembering the "achievable" in SMART. Either schedule one task toward your goal each day or choose a day of the week on which you'll knock off several of those tasks.

Planning your week and sticking to the plan is another crucial aspect of setting goals effectively.

CHECK-IN WITH YOURSELF EACH WEEK

When the week's over, it's time to check in with yourself to see how you've done.

Reflecting on your ability to meet the goals you've set and complete the tasks associated with them on time is how you keep yourself honest. That honesty is the jet fuel that propels you toward your purpose.

And when you've achieved all, you've set out to do, celebrate! Congratulate yourself. Share your success with those closest to you. Achievements are worthy of celebration because they require a lot of discipline and focus to realize, which is why many people can't quite get themselves to do it!

But you're doing it, so celebrate the small victories. Those little battles you win are steppingstones toward what you've decided to do with your life.

So, there you are. You're awake, and it's 5 am. But what's your morning routine? Let's discuss that next.

YOUR MORNING ROUTINE

The morning is your most productive time. Well, maybe not yet—but it's going to be!

My recommendation—and I live by it—is to give yourself at least 2 hours for the morning routine, which will be the foundation of living your purpose.

You'll have plenty you'll want to get done in those two hours, and while it sounds like a lot of time, you'll find you wish you had even more time.

Who knows, maybe you'll become an early riser in the order of Tim Cook, Apple CEO, who starts his day at 3:45 am.

Baby steps, for now, right?

Here's my formula for an early morning routine that grounds you, gets you ahead of your daily game, and moves you forward.

VAT—VISUALIZATION, AFFIRMATIONS, AND THANKSGIVING

Allot 12 minutes to this part of your routine. And remember, you'll have days when you only have an hour for the various activities in your morning routine. All you need to do is cut the time allotted in half. Contingencies happen, so have a plan.

Visualization is one of the most helpful goal-oriented activities you can use. It's said that if you can see yourself doing something, you can do it. Visualize yourself knocking tasks off your weekly list and achieving the goals you've set. How does that make you feel? Great, right?

Affirmations are another valuable goal-directed skill. Here's where you encourage yourself! You know what you've got to offer the world, so tell yourself that, whatever that may be. It's incredible! Make firm, explicit statements about yourself, like:

> "I am creating the life I deserve."
> "I am becoming the best I can be."
> "I will reach all my goals today, tomorrow, and all days."
> "I will keep going until I'm where I know I need to be."

And finally, you're going to give Thanks—in advance—for reaching your goals.

Giving thanks reminds us that nothing comes to us without our engagement. It also reminds us that gratitude is the mark of someone who understands the fragility of human experiences, is not arrogant, and applies humility to all they do. Humility is a leadership quality that top-level employers increasingly seek out.

MINDFULNESS MEDITATION

Most people's heads are full of racing thoughts in the morning. They're thinking through what's on the docket for the day and mentally preparing themselves.

But there's a much better way to prepare yourself for what's on tap. Mindfulness meditation is the practice of slowing your mind down, which has the effect of relaxing the body.

Focus on where you are in the moment and allow your thoughts to drift through with no judgment or commentary from you. This allows you to just "be."

All you need is a comfortable place to sit and a posture that frees you to breathe slowly and comfortably. Give yourself an allowance of 30 minutes for this portion of your routine.

EXERCISE

Exercise is something everyone should be doing. I strongly suggest that you find a way to exercise at home as part of your morning routine, to cut down on time required to achieve it.

Choose a type of exercise that appeals to you. Maybe one of your personal development goals is to learn Yoga or Pilates, or another kind of exercise. I exercise in my living room, and I follow a routine that combines body weight exercises with a high- repetition, a light-weights routine, and some calisthenics. You may prefer a stationary cycle or a rowing machine.

Whatever you choose, know that your body will feel cared for and prepared for the day when you're done. You've got 18 minutes for this part of your morning routine, so make them count!

WORK ON YOUR GOALS

I hope you've already prioritized your goals because now, you're going to start working on them in order of priority.

These can be either long or short-term goals. But long-term goals are well served by alert morning time. Putting them in your morning routine lets you immerse yourself in the future you're building.

Read books that aren't part of the curriculum for your field of study, but which shed light and a broader view on the subject. This will bolster your position in your class by improving your performance and your grade.

Maybe one of your long-term goals is executing a business idea you've been pondering. One of your other long-term goals could be achieving total financial freedom by the age of 30. The business idea you're aiming to bring to life could be your strategy.

That's a twofer!

And it's also a great goal to shoot for. Creating an independent lifestyle is the only real security we can hope for in this world.

When we captain our own ships, there's no one else to point fingers at when the ship sinks.

And the ship is less likely to sink with you at the helm – right?

That's what working on your goals as part of your morning routine is all about – long-term goals that will help you get to the life you're striving for. With that in mind, be clear and deliberate about your goals.

Then, be relentless about working toward them every morning. This activity will need 36 minutes.

REVIEW

This is the part of your morning routine set aside for taking a peek at your goals but in a completely different way. You should be able to blow through it in 24 minutes or less if nothing changes. Life turns on a dime, and our outlooks and feelings change as we take in new information. Conditions change (see: COVID-19).

Naturally, change requires being honest with ourselves to adjust our goals—especially our long-term goals—accordingly.

This ability is essential, as change is inevitable. You don't only need to build that understanding into your matrix of goals but also your worldview. When fostered early in life, Adaptability is a critical leadership quality that will serve you well irrespective of your profession.

Change affects everything, so look at your short-term goals too. Anything can happen. Maybe you're aware of a condition on the event horizon that's directly in the way of one of these immediate goals. That condition is teaching you a valuable lesson about life. Some of us live our entire lives and never learn it, and others only learn to accept it. But those who live their lives authentically embrace change and make it part of the way they live their lives.

Round out your morning routine with a look at the day ahead. You'll be in classes but which classes? Are you prepared? Have you gone the extra mile? Are you worthy of the high grade you want?

This last part of your day is what you've been preparing for because it's in the review portion of your morning routine that you begin to engage with the day ahead. You're already moving and not running a hand through your hair and dashing out the door; you're calmly reviewing what's ahead.

Now, go. Take a shower and go forth to face the day with conviction!

In the next chapter, we're going deeper into the morning routine, with a detailed discussion of each element involved.

3

THE "WHYS" AND "WHEREFORES" OF THE MORNING ROUTINE

Now that we've gone through the morning routine framework, you may be asking yourself why I've created it in this way. That's a fair question, and in this chapter, I will answer it in detail.

It's my wish that you fully understand the significance and benefit of the early-rising lifestyle. So, you must understand why I've offered these specific actions as part of the morning routine.

Let's get a closer look at the nuts and bolts of the morning routine that will propel you forward!

VAT (VISUALIZATION, AFFIRMATION AND GIVING THANKS IN ADVANCE)

The VAT part of your morning routine is an intentional preparation of your mind for the coming day.

In this section, I'll break the acronym down to its constituent parts and discuss them separately, starting with "V."

VISUALIZATION

Nothing in the world that human hands ever made was not first seen in the mind's eye. Think about it. Inventions of all kinds have their origin in Visualization.

So, applying the creative process of Visualization to your goals allows you to see their completion beforehand. In that ability lies great power.

If you can imagine yourself making or doing something, it's much more likely that you'll be able to replicate those actions in real life.

The first component of Visualization is intentionality. You and I can certainly agree that we visualize all the time. We fixate on worst-case scenarios, rehearse what we'll say to the boss, or place ourselves on a distant tropical beach.

But none of these examples is genuinely intentional, and it's intentionality that makes visualizing your goals effective.

The next component is **process**.

This is when you visualize the steps required to reach the goal you're focusing on in your Visualization. For example, you want to speak French, so you can find a course near where you live, work, or online. You enroll.

You take the classes, move to the intermediate level course, and finally to the advanced level. You speak conversational French. Maybe you go on to learn an even higher level for your studies, travel, or business.

But as you visualize, you're moving through each step and imagining your progress.

Outcome is the next component. Here's where all the steps result in the realization of the goal in mind. Like the steps towards completing goals, the steps in Visualization lead you to a conclusion – the outcome.

And the outcome you're looking for is **success**. So don't take the role of a passive observer. This is not an out-of-body experience. It's more like being there and, through your own eyes, seeing the experience as it happens around you.

Detail is vital in Visualization, as your brain will begin to make connections, which lead to sharpened performance and heightened motivation, according to Jennice Vilhauer, Ph.D., writing for Psychology Today. She further points out that the more you think about something, the greater its significance in your mental landscape.

For example, you'd love to eat a burger right now. But you're at work and can't leave, so you dismiss the thought. But what if you dwell on that tasty burger? Imagine its juicy, charbroiled goodness, hot off the grill? Envision the ketchup dripping from beneath the bun and down the patty's flank, and the fries that come with it, crispy and golden? Can you taste it?

In the last instance, you'll likely crawl to the next town for that burger and fries, right? That's because of the detail of your Visualization. The true success of Visualization is in seeing every possible detail of what you're focusing on.

The details create an emotional landscape in the Visualization and a connection between you and the goal.

Every detail creates a type of virtual reality that makes your goal as real as the chair you're sitting on.

That realness means that you're positioning yourself to the goal and action involved in.

Visualization is a powerful tool that brings your goals into focus, creating a deep bond between you and the life you've planned for yourself. You invest when you visualize effectively, and in that investment are material returns.

BEFORE YOU BEGIN

This is the first activity of your morning routine, and if you are just starting, chances are you might still feel sleepy. It's you just being human, and I get it. So how about we start by addressing this.

Your objective at this point is to increase your level of wakefulness to as close to 99.99% as possible. The good news is, you already took some steps towards that by getting at least 7 hours of sleep, meaning you are well-rested. Next thing, you got your entire body in motion by getting completely out of bed to reach and turn off the 5 am alarm.

The next insanely vital thing to do to keep the motion going is to *walk* to the kitchen or wherever you have your drinking water stored. Drink 2 cups (16 ounces) of room temperature water. The walk will help keep you awake and drinking water first thing in the morning as you wake up is an essential act of self-love to reverse the dehydration of a night's sleep. So that's a twofer right there. Let's digress here for a bit because I believe it all works together- if the engine of a vehicle is not working efficiently, then I think the trip may altogether be flawed. Here are four reasons you should drink water first thing in the morning after waking up:

1) Improve your digestion efficiency.

This works even better with warm water. It will help break down the food in your stomach even faster, making it more digestible.

2) Lose weight.

Consuming water first thing in the morning increases your metabolism, which goes a long way to help your body burn more calories. It's ok to squeeze some fresh lemon juice in it, which will also help with weight loss.

3) Cure illnesses and diseases.

Studies carried out at the University of Sydney showed that drinking water first thing in the morning lowers the risk of you suffering from kidney disease. Drinking water throughout the day helps flush toxins from your body, reducing your risk of contracting life-threatening diseases such as high blood pressure and diabetes.

4) Rehydration.

After sleeping for a minimum of 7 hours, your body will be dehydrated, especially if you did not drink water before going to bed. Given the importance of water in our system, the logical thing to do is to rehydrate when you wake up.

Phew! That was quite a bit, wasn't it :)? Now that I have gotten how to stay awake after rising from bed out of the way, let us talk Visualization, step by step now.

Your step one will be to choose a goal and plot your Visualization out in writing. Think of this as a screenplay for a movie or an outline for a book. Throwing yourself into Visualization without performing this step is tempting but know this: your Visualization won't be as effective if you don't write it down first.

Here's why: simply, our minds wander.

You know that. I know that; everybody knows that. Our active minds are full of fleeting, random thoughts and imagery.

Getting sidetracked by these inconsequential thoughts—like breakfast, random worries, or negative thoughts—undermines the whole process.

Writing it down gives you something concrete to follow. You are the author/director of your Visualization, and you're not about to let breakfast wander onto your set narrative.

Step two is to write down the emotions you believe you'll feel after you've realized the goal. Write down these emotions—pride in yourself, gratitude, happiness according to what you know about yourself. As you identify the projected emotions, you'll begin to feel excited. Connecting in this way with your goals propels you into the action associated with them. It's in our emotional life that we find that passion, which translates into success. Visualization might even be thought of as a sneak preview of the purpose-driven life you are building!

Your third and last step of visualizing the achievement of your goal(s) is to *relax and breathe*. It doesn't matter whether you lay down or sit down in an upright position, so long as no one will disturb you—which is unlikely at 5 am. You are already in comfortable clothes, so no worries there. However, you face the risk of risk falling back to sleep if you do this. So be smart.

Once you are comfortable, take a moment to slow your breathing down, breathing in for five counts at average speed and then out for five. Do five rounds of these. Breath from your diaphragm by expanding your abdomen on the inhale and relaxing on the exhale. This will ensure you fill your lungs with each breathe.

As you breathe, your body will relax.

If you feel any tension in any part of your body, focus on it as you breathe. Feel that part of your body relaxing. Sense your blood flowing through it and feel your breath flowing in and out of your body.

Once relaxed, it's time to embark on the adventure of visualizing your goal, feel the emotion.

AFFIRMATION

The practice of affirmation has become incredibly popular. And that's kind of a miracle, as many people find it a little weird to say beautiful things about themselves.

But we must!

We need to believe in our purpose and goals, and what we have planned for our lives. For this to happen, we need to be confident in our ability to realize those plans.

It is crucial then to understand that affirmation is a scientifically supported practice with significant evidentiary support. Permit me to share a few with you below. Hang in there.

NEUROSCIENCE AND AFFIRMATION

In his book, The Brain That Changes Itself: Stories of Personal Triumph from the Frontiers of Brain Science, a psychiatrist, and researcher, Dr. Norman Doidge, relates the findings of a study in which two groups were asked to exercise a particular finger muscle. One group did the actual exercise, and the other group only visualized doing it.

The group that did the exercise saw muscle strength increase by 30%, on average. The visualization group saw a 22% increase. That is a pretty impressive result, don't you think? It certainly is, and what undergirds affirmation as a daily practice is empirically supported as well.

A study published in the Oxford Journal of Cognitive and Affective Neuroscience has confirmed that affirmation fires up the systems in the brain associated with reward. To prove this, researchers employed functional magnetic resonance imagery (fMRI).

Using this diagnostic tool, the brain's reward centers—ventral striatum and ventromedial prefrontal cortex—the part of the brain that responds when we experience pleasure—researchers observed increased activity resulting from the practice of affirmation.

Additionally, affirmations were observed to provoke and increase activity in the two parts of the brain governing self-related processing—the posterior cingulate and the medial prefrontal cortex. Self-related processing is how you respond to threats, pain, and negativity. It's the brain's way of creating a buffer zone between your mental health and the stressful information it's responding to.

Another result of this study is that affirmations stated in the future tense provoked greater spikes in the brain regions discussed above than those stated in the past or present. An example might be:

"I will soon be a formidable presence in my chosen field."

A future-based statement was observed to fire up the brain's reward centers and centers of self-related processing more than a statement like this might:

"I've been excellent at my job, and I'll be better at it tomorrow."

Casting your affirmation in the future tense takes your Visualization to the next level by enhancing activity in areas of the brain that make you feel good. And feeling good is something everyone wants. When you feel good mentally, your physical health is sure to follow. It's not only that; your positive attitude and energy are attributes employers seek. Affirmations can help you grow into a leader.

YOUR BRAIN CAN BE TRAINED

Think of affirmations as factual statements, confidently spoken. Affirmations play an essential role in realizing your purpose and goal-supportive activities. Practicing Visualization and affirmations repeatedly rewires your brain and demonstrates your confidence in the statement.

Over time, practicing affirmations with Visualization helps realize the goal.

Every one of us remembers an instance—or many instances in childhood of being told we couldn't do this or that. Someone in our history delightfully took it upon themselves to make sure that we would never so much as attempt whatever we were being told we couldn't do.

And that's probably why so many of us have a problem with affirmations. Negative feedback is often some-one's opinion based on their own assumptions. There may be a little envy thrown in for good measure and usually, a dash of a need to control you. In his book, Becoming Supernatural, Dr. Joe Dispenza demonstrates how our thoughts influence our feelings and how these feelings influence our thoughts. He called it the thinking and feeling loop. So, mind what you think, especially about yourself.

Affirmations banish this negativity from our minds so that we can use them more effectively. A lack of confidence serves no one, and it nails your feet to the floor. Affirming your goals and purpose affirms you, allowing you to free your feet to move and your brain to achieve.

Affirmations still the voices in the past that we too often cling to. Those voices ruin lives. Affirmations heal them and crown them with success.

ARRIVING AT YOUR AFFIRMATIONS

Now that you understand why it works, let's get to it. The essential part of creating affirmations is to come up with statements directly related to your actions and your abilities.

Also, remember to filter out anything that is even remotely negative. This is about making your brain a happy, cooperative camper.

And remember what you previously read about the neuroscience of affirmations—the future tense is powerful.

Make affirmations rooted in the present but be aware that your brain responds most fulsomely when you provoke activity in your brain's reward centers and areas associated with the future (hippocampus). Especially at the beginning, activate these potently with future-oriented affirmations.

Your affirmations are not epic novels, so keep them to one sentence. Be deliberate about what you're creating and keep it simple. The simpler it is, the better it's going to do what you want it to.

Don't leave your emotions out of it either. Your affirmations must refer to emotions and how the affirmation itself interacts with them.

For example:

> "I am going to be so proud when I've achieved
> this goal."
> That's more effective than saying:
> "I am going to achieve this goal."

Evoking emotional states also targets a result. You're naming an outcome you desire, and your emotions at resolution are a big part of it.

An affirmation is like a bodyweight exercise; only it's for your brain. You're giving it an unequivocal statement. Your brain knows how to interpret self-talk only as reality. Thus affirmations mold desired results.

As you state your affirmations, looking in a mirror at yourself isn't a bad idea, but you needn't. The way it works is that the words, when repeated regularly, become the brain's reality, and it is your truth.

You are the master of your destiny—I needn't tell you. But you are also the master of your brain, and a discipline of daily affirmations tells it who is running the show.

GIVING THANKS IN ADVANCE

Gratitude has a transformative power on our lives, which can't be understated. So, why are we such ungrateful people?

We're rarely happy with anything, always wanting more, better, and bigger. We want to be first in line for this, that, and the other thing. We are an entitled group of people.

But giving thanks in advance changes everything.

Martin Seligman, a Positive Psychologist, studied positive emotions such as gratitude, altruism, optimism, compassion, happiness, and forgiveness and their effects on our brains.

Psychologists before him had almost exclusively studied negative emotions such as mental illness, behavior and cognition trauma, addiction, stress, and anxiety.

Seligman's work was continued in 2007 by Robert Emmons, who was interested in looking at how gratitude affected psychology. Emmons' work revealed a strong co-relationship between gratitude and quality of life, mental health, and overall satisfaction.

HOW YOU CAN INCREASE GRATITUDE

It may sound a little crazy, but expressing your gratitude in advance of achieving a goal conforms to what we read earlier about affirmations set in the future. Here, you're not affirming yourself. You're saying 'Thank you' for the satisfaction derived from the realization of your goals, modeling humility that grows you into a better version of yourself.

Expressing your gratitude before receiving a positive result is really about faith. It's faith in yourself that allows you to be humble enough to admit that the world does not revolve around you. You are not the sun. You are someone the sun shines down upon—one more thing to be grateful for!

The things we do every day to improve ourselves have the most significant effect on our outlook. Hence, daily expression of gratitude increases your ability to continue those improvements and thus keep feeling grateful.

Give thanks for the achievement of your goals and your purpose in life. If you're shooting for a 4.0 GPA, expressing gratitude acknowledges one thing: the fact that you're working hard to achieve it.

Try something like:

"I give thanks for the 4.0 GPA I'll achieve."
Or,
"I give thanks for the satisfaction I feel from realizing my life's purpose."
Next, let's examine the value of mindfulness meditation in your morning routine.

MINDFULNESS MEDITATION

I hope the teaser about mindfulness meditation has whet your appetite for more. Nothing worth having is instant, and you'll need time and familiarity with the practice of mindfulness meditation to receive optimal benefit from it.

If you've never tried a meditation discipline, then be kind to yourself. Start small. Start with 5 minutes, then build slowly toward mastery. I strongly recommend that you spend 25% of your morning routine time on this. If you're starting with five minutes, allot the time to other items in the routine framework. Use the time well.

Give mindfulness meditation your time and be richly rewarded. It has changed my life!

Modern life is a twitchy, restless affair. Many of our human minds spend an excessive amount of time nervously toggling between yesterday's disappointments, today's pressures, and the future's uncertainty.

That means we're never where we need to be, which is in the present. Mindfulness meditation trains you to be present.

When your mind is rooted in the present, you don't just passively hear. You actively listen. You don't just allow the world to drift over and under and around as you obsess. You are part of the world and its living experience, and you are present.

If you're new to mindfulness meditation, here's a summary of how to get yourself to that special place known as "now." When you're centered and living in the present, you'll see things as they are.

Stressed out and always anxious about your academic performance? Feel lonely, sad, and depressed sometimes? Trust me. I've been there, and I know exactly what it feels like. The good news is, you'll feel less so with this discipline.

You'll be more focused and attentive and find that you're able to concentrate more readily. Also, you'll understand and be able to manage your emotions better.

Your emotional intelligence—the foundation of outstanding leadership—will increase. You'll be better at drawing people who don't agree with each other together because you'll enhance your empathy and respect for others. You will feel better and be able to manage whatever comes your way with grace. But if you are an Arts Major, look out! Your creativity will burgeon!

THE PRACTICE OF MINDFULNESS MEDITATION

The following strategies practiced routinely will make you a master of mindfulness meditation.

- Choose a space you'll use every day for this purpose. Choose well because entering your meditation space will prime you for what you're about to do. This space can be in your bedroom, living room, or any place that's available quiet and where you'll not be disturbed.

- Choose the proper posture. Not everybody is comfortable in a Lotus position. If you feel that lying down makes it easier to be in the 'now,' go ahead. But you risk falling asleep, which is not what we want, do we? My recommendation, which I currently practice, is to sit in an upright position on a regular chair, feet flat on the floor, and sit in an upright position. This will keep your spine straight and will keep most people awake. Gently place your palms on your thighs and close your eyes. I have found that when I close my eyes, my meditation is more effective because it eliminates visual distractions. But it's ok to have them open if you choose to.

- The bottom line is, choose a technique that suits you. But also, be intentional about what's around you and how you're approaching your meditation session. Focus on your breath. Slow it down.

Place items in your meditation space that serve your practice, if possible. A candle, incense, a beautiful image

– all these can help but are not a requirement at all. I also imagine you are in a dorm room and might be sharing the space with someone else. So be considerate of what your roommate/s will tolerate.

- Set a timer before you begin, so it beeps at the end of the allotted time for this part of the routine-30 minutes. Set a shorter timeframe and start small if you are a beginner adding increments of 5 minutes.
- You are seated and ready to begin. Place your palms on your thighs and release the tension in your arms. Let the tension go and say the word "relax".
- Once again, take in those deep breathes, counting from 1 to 5 at an average pace as you inhale and exhale. Repeat four times more to get five rounds in total.
- Slowly return to your normal breathing rhythm and focus on it. Feel the air sensation through your nostrils as you inhale and the warm air sensation as you exhale. You will notice random thoughts flow into your mind. This is perfectly normal. Acknowledge stray thoughts without passing judgment or responding to them with another thought. They are like passengers on the train or bus. Simply find your way to the

present moment by returning your focus to your breathing.

- You might feel an itch or two on a part of your body. Try to sit with it without scratching for as long as you can-even 2 seconds. It will help enforce your ability to be patient in life and not give in to instant gratification very quickly.
- Keep on redirecting your awareness to your breathing when your mind wanders. Before you know it, 30 minutes will have gone by as peacefully as a dove soaring through the blue skies. This, my friend, is the mindful meditation phase of your morning routine.
- After 30 minutes or so of being physically motionless for the most part, it is time to get those bones and muscles moving.

EXERCISE

Many health experts with an interest in preventative and supportive health practices have weighed in on physical exercise. Their position is that you'll have a better, healthier, and more satisfying life if you exercise regularly.

Let's talk about the benefits of getting active, staying active, and making exercise a regular part of your life.

Here, I'll review critical demographics and appropriate exercise levels for each. I'm doing it this way because many of us tend to abandon exercise as we age. The results of this reality can be seen out in the streets of our towns and cities. Obesity, shortness of breath, heart diseases, diabetes, fatigue, and a host of other health complications can be remedied by daily exercise. The following can serve as a life tool to check what exercise you should be doing as you age.

As you read, understand that it is assumed you have no underlying health conditions. If you have one, you should be talking to your doctor about how and what exercises will be most suitable for you.

18 and 19-year-olds

If you are a freshman or freshwoman, chances are that you, my friend, are in this age group. Here are my thoughts and recommendations for you:

- The blush of childhood still colors your cheeks, so you're well placed to start an exercise habit that will support you throughout your life if you haven't started already. This is almost the best age to form the habit of exercise in your mind and your life, so it becomes a need you feel.
- Do you play a competitive sport? No? Time to

start. Your ultra-youthful body can do anything, so find the sport you're most attracted to and do it.

- Get moving. Put the cell phone down, turn off the computer and get moving. Sitting all day is not good for your body or brain. Now is the time to learn to incorporate movement into your day and life. The Surgeon General of the US calls sitting the new smoking. It's as damaging to the body. Even apart from routine workouts, it's important to get up and move a few minutes every two hours.

- For your morning routine, focus on efficient exercises that get the job done while maximizing your time. Bodyweight exercises are ideal. Try planks (there are several varieties, so learn a couple) and hip bridging. Calisthenics (jumping jacks, pushups, squats, lunges) are also efficient, self-contained exercises. Exercises that challenge your entire body (e.g. cardio) are time-efficient and exceptionally effective. Yoga poses are also excellent for this purpose. Mix them up to achieve a full-body exercise.

- Remember that the good habits you form now are those you'll likely maintain all your life. As you get older, you'll need to change your routine to accommodate physical changes and support them with the best medicine there is—exercise.

20-Somethings

- Your 20s are a golden time. You will never be more energetic and healthier than you are right now. What better time to start leveraging that advantage to carry yourself through life better prepared to meet its challenges? Also, if you are new to routine exercise, you'll find it only adds to your energy level.
- If you don't play a sport, you might want to start.
- Tennis and racquetball are ideal for people in their 20s, as it demands physical exertion of the entire body, especially the cardiovascular system.
- In fact, at your age, anything is good. Bike, hike, dance, pump iron – it's all good exercise for people of your age, for whom daily exercise is a must.
- For your morning routine, just as with the teens, focus on bodyweight exercises is also fine. Planks, hip bridging, calisthenics, spot jogs, lunges, squats, tuck jumps, jumping jacks, and stretches are great.

- Training your mind and body to crave exercise is easy. The more *consistent* you are, the better the results will be.

30-Somethings

- Once you 'hit' 30, you are entering the age of physical decline, as some say(tough to accept, I know). But you're adding exercise to your daily routine, which will go a long way toward maintaining your health and fitness.
- People in their 30s are already losing muscle mass and bone, which will continue throughout their lives, making them vulnerable to osteoporosis. According to The American Society for Bone and Mineral Research, annual fractures and costs are projected to rise by almost 50% by 2025.
- Imagine being 40 or 50 and never having exercised in your entire life. Imagine that you've never so much as walked further than a mile. That's a recipe for potential disaster.
- Focusing on bone and muscle strength in your 30s is a winning strategy. Weight training, resistance bands, and bodyweight exercises will build your muscles and bones, making you infinitely more physically resilient. Dancing or

step aerobics, hiking, jogging/running, jumping rope, stair climbing, and tennis are great exercises.

- Experiment with your workouts. Switch them. Try Pilates – ideal for your age group's needs. Challenge your muscles by using different movements and performing varied activities. Changing your routine will also keep you engaged with the goal of feeling well throughout your life.

- For your morning routine, pick a couple of exercises that are most convenient for you and do them. Have in mind the time allotted for this section of the morning routine. To start seeing results, consistency is key. That is why it must be done daily.

40-Somethings

- Here's where the going gets heavy. Stopping on continuing a lifestyle of no exercise at this age is a set-up for disease and stress. This is the decade in which underlying conditions begin to trouble people. Not exercising, eating healthily, or intentionally caring for your physical needs can take a tremendous toll by your 40s.

- But you're not going to let that happen because

you're already on it! Your 40s are going to be fabulous because I know you'll keep it up!

- Worst of all, people in their 40s begin to fall prey to slowing metabolisms, causing them to gain weight quickly.
- Hormone levels begin to decline, and tendons and ligaments stiffen. Joints start acting up, and before they know it, it's hip replacement time!
- 40-somethings need to be carefully dedicated to following a daily exercise routine. Weight-bearing exercise should be balanced with adequate cardio to support your heart and lungs while caring for your bone and muscle mass. See recommendations for 30 somethings to build bone and muscle mass.

50-Somethings

- The quality of life you enjoy in your 50s is directly attributable to your lifelong habits. If one of those habits were exercise, you'd most likely fare well during this decade. If it wasn't, it might hurt! But it's never too late to achieve the benefits of exercise if you then.
- Most people in their 50s face health challenges, but you can minimize potential problems and perhaps avoid them with exercise.

- Aches and pains you could never have imagined arise, but that doesn't imply that you can't exercise. Try low-impact exercise – walking, swimming, cycling, elliptical training, and swimming fit that bill.

- And here's where you need to mind your posture. Your body will tend to lean forward as you age, and you may find your poking chin and shoulders curving forward. You can alleviate this by building up the muscles in your core (mid-section). Engaging your abdomen, back, and gluteal muscles all serve better posture in your 50s.

- My number one pick for the most efficient, whole-body exercise of all time is the plank. In only 2 minutes, you work the core, shoulders, hamstrings, and calves.

- I strongly suggest that you develop this exercise by watching good tutorials (I would advise some good sources for tutorials as not all are good reliable sources). NIH is a good one, or finding a coach to help with planks and other valuable bodyweight exercises that suit people in their 50s to a "t."

60-somethings

- If you've been exercising all your life diligently, your 60s won't be scary.
- Exercise is a magical ingredient that preserves mobility in the joints, keeps excess weight off, and makes you feel much younger.
- Once you've reached your 60s and exercise has been your constant companion through life, you'll be able to keep going. Routines that include weights – including bodyweight exercises, as described earlier – are beneficial for people in their 60s since muscle atrophy can become a severe problem in this decade of life.
- Yoga, Pilates, bicycle riding, swimming, and fast walking are all excellent options for your 60s.

70-somethings

- Once you've made it to your 70s, you'll be the fittest, healthiest person around if you've stayed true to the human body's need for exercise.
- Resistance bands, also called "Pilates" bands these days, are a fantastic addition to your workout equipment for this decade. Resistance bands allow you to challenge muscles,

ligaments, and tendons while controlling the action.

- Tai chi, a style of exercise that hails from China, is an enormously popular type of exercise for people who've arrived in their 70s. Gentle and low-impact, Tai Chi's movements encourage balance – often an issue for older people – and strengthening.
- But there's a meditative aspect to the form of internal martial arts that heightens the slow, gentle movements.

80+

- Moderate aerobic exercise should account for about 80% of your exercise routine once you reach your 80s. Your heart and lungs will get a boost from activities like fast walking, cycling, or swimming.
- 20% of your exercise routine should be devoted to resistance training – see the section on resistance bands, under "20-somethings". But using the weight of your body is another way to train your muscles and maintain a healthy, upright posture. So, keep those planks and hip bridges coming! The NIH website is a place to go for the correct form.

WORKING ON YOUR GOALS

Now that you've prioritized your goals, it's time to get to work!

Your morning routine demands that goals be at the front of your mind. This is your time to build the foundation for your future and assemble a list of prioritized goals as you deem fit and central to your success.

- Read a book that improves your knowledge in your course load. Pump up your education by seeking out reading materials outside the curriculum. You're a warrior.
- Work on an idea you have. That could be a business, a foundation, or a support network. But your business idea may well be the way forward to achieving the financial freedom we all desire. Think about your goals in terms of self-actualization and gaining freedom from economic stressors, which severely impact many people.

REVIEW

This is the part of your morning routine in which you revisit your goals. Don't be afraid to adjust for contingencies and other unexpected conditions. Knowing that anything can happen and organizing your goals with that in mind will lead to flexibility and poise in your professional life. Your goals change over time as you do.

Following your goal/purpose review, plan your day. You'll be seeing which classes are up and where you need to be on campus, club meetings, and other daily priorities. This will allow you to work through your day unruffled and prepared calmly.

4

WAKING UP IS HARD TO DO!

Humans are creatures of habit.

W e tend not to care much for change, so many of us respond to any change as a threat.

"There is nothing permanent except change"

— HERACLITUS

Life changes. Priorities change. Students are in a profound state of change and development, so fostering that ability is part of why you want to rise at 5 a.m. Being ready for change, expecting it, is a life skill. Still, adapting to change well is also a professional aptitude that employers value and the society requires to function optimally.

Part of what you're about to learn concerns the shift from being a night owl to an early riser.

WHY WE FEAR CHANGE

While humans are creatures of habit, we're also quite adaptable. Many of us just prefer not to adapt, and we're content with things as they are. Many of us and others don't know what is required to adapt well to a changing world.

Change presents itself to our instinct-based thinking as an existential threat. We don't know what to expect from change or how it will affect our lives as we understand them.

But in the face of change, we feel a profound sense of potential extinction in the pit of our stomachs. That may be a bit dramatic, but the primitive lizard brain tends to be a bit of a drama queen. The primitive lizard brain is wired to respond to change with fear. Even if the prevailing conditions aren't ideal or even undesirable, we prefer to resist change.

A study conducted in 2016 by a team of researchers explored the relationship between uncertainty and stress. Physical symptoms like sweating and pupil dilation were examined to gauge stress levels physiologically. The study found an intimate connection, following these physical signs, between uncertainty and increased stress.

When dopamine is released, the brain's striatum (part of the brain's "reward center) responds. But the striatum can also predict the level of uncertainty involved. When that level hits 50%, the flag turns red and physical symptoms like breaking out in a cold sweat occur. You're now in "fight or flight" mode.

And we admire those who "have it all under control." We want to be able to order our lives so ideally that they become bullet-proof.

But that's impossible. Understanding that life is a change from start to finish is probably the best message you can absorb when embracing change. It's not easy, but it's necessary, and you know that because you're here.

GETTING OVER IT

One of the biggest psychological roadblocks you need to overcome is fear of failure. As I've said earlier, failure is a teacher, and we shouldn't fear failure because it's a stepping stone to success.

Failure creates an opportunity to examine the mechanics of what went wrong. Deconstructing failure is the answer to success, and giving up is not.

Life can be uncertain. Nothing in life is guaranteed, even factoring in our best efforts. Wars break out; systems break down, pandemics happen. Even our best-laid plans won't get us past contingencies like these. We need strategies to get past the roadblocks.

The first strategy is to accept the uncertainty, always remembering that life is best lived fearlessly.

Learning how to get over the fear of failure and uncertainty is one of the greatest gifts you'll ever give yourself. Do something exciting for yourself. Part of that excitement is launching yourself into a new enterprise without knowing how it will all end.

If you want the life you've dreamed of, you must work on conquering fear and uncertainty.

Additional strategies to help you include:

- **Put the past in the past.** This is your life now. Your life will have chapters that end to start the next. Before you can effectively start something new, you must put the past away.

- **Be decisive.** The decisions you make now will create your future. Your life is being written as you live it. You are the author. Decide how to navigate the plot twists.

- **Accept imperfections.** If what you're shooting for is perfection, you're going to be sorely disappointed. So, release perfectionism.

- **Accept that you have no control over the thoughts or actions of others.** As irritating as it is, you must accept that people will think and do what they want to think and do. Even when what they do is annoying or the worst possible move for them, your attempt to intervene will almost always fail and met with resentment. That said, say your piece, and then move on. You might exert influence but the choice to change is theirs. Move on after speaking your mind.

CREATING HABITS THAT STICK

There's no point in creating new habits unless they are good ones, and you intend to make them stick.

Creating positive habits is a four-step process:

The Cue

The cue initiates the four-part sequence. It refers to something that triggers an action, your emotional state, or a location. As new habits form, the cue becomes automatic and signals to your brain and body to perform the action that becomes your new habit.

The Craving

Cravings move us. They are the reason we act. Having been cued to the proximity of a reward, we come to crave it—we want to perform the action that leads to a reward. You crave the reward of realizing your purpose by reaching your goals, so you're going to start rising at 5 a.m. to get it.

The Response

Your goal is to use the cue to respond to a lasting, positive habit mindfully. And you can only form a habit that you can sustain. That's why all those New Year's resolutions to lose weight and get buff dissipate by the beginning of February. The sustainability of an action has to be factored in. Can you sustainably manage your new norma—rising at 5 a.m. and taking all the steps required to reach your goals and, eventually, your purpose?

The Reward

A sustained response is how you get the reward. Every habit you form now is a habit that will deliver a reward. We want to be rewarded for the satisfaction of having achieved a goal and learning how to sustain it.

Every step of the process must be satisfied to get to the reward. If you ignore cues/triggers, there will be no reward. If you ignore that craving to perform the actions required by the 5 a.m. lifestyle, there will be no reward.

Expect no overnight miracles.

Forming positive habits takes an average of 21 days. If you maintain a behavior for 21 days, you have likely formed a habit that will stick.

You've discovered you CAN do it.

The habit is, therefore, sustainable.

In your case, as a student, rising at 5 a.m. will deliver endless rewards as you move through life.

BESPOKE IT

The trick to forming the habit of rising at 5 a.m. is to ensure that the habit is sustainable. Part of assuring that is safeguarding the amount of sleep you get each night.

Rising at 5 a.m. is not at all sustainable unless you're getting 7-8 hours of sleep each night—we'll talk about that more shortly. You are trying to tap into the early morning hours' clarity and quiet to foster a complex of behaviors that lead to success. You're not helping yourself if you get out of bed tired, so learn to go to bed earlier. It will become second nature in a matter of 3 short weeks. Not bad, for a better, more satisfying life.

Remembering that Rome wasn't built in a day, **ease yourself into an early morning routine**. If you're a habitual late riser, get up 15 minutes earlier to start. Then half an hour. Then 45 minutes. You can do it the same way on the other end until you are consistently going to bed at a time that enables you to get the amount of sleep you need and rise at 5 a.m. Continue until you've recalibrated your wake/sleep cycle.

And **move that alarm clock**! The snooze button must be far out of reach if you're going to succeed at earlier rising.

The **minute the alarm sounds, you rub your eyes, roll out of bed, and** get a drink of water I earlier talked about to stay awake. Lingering only makes your bed more tempting.

Don't bargain with yourself.

Stick to your guns and quiet the little voice that whines about returning to bed to shut up.

If you like a sleep-in, you have a free day. This is the one day per week that you can indulge in your desire to sleep later. Be intentional about getting there by looking forward to it and luxuriating in it. Don't deny yourself this reward because you earned it! You should be smart about how later you go to bed because it could adversely impact your ability to resume rising early.

SEVEN HOURS THAT MEAN SO MUCH

Getting up early is hard. But going to bed earlier can be challenging too. When we can get these two right, the rest falls into place.

I already established in these pages that most adults under the age of 65 need at least seven hours of sleep each night. This is now your mission. You need those 7 to 9 hours of sleep, not only to get up and pursue your morning routine, but to be at your most productive and alert throughout the day.

SLEEP CYCLES

To understand why you need at least seven hours of sleep each night, you must know how many sleep cycles you go through in those 7 hours. According to the National Sleep Foundation, there are two sleep cycles: REM and non-REM sleep. REM sleep is when you dream. This type of sleep serves learning and memory and is most restorative. As a student, you need REM Sleep! Most adults move through 5 or 6 sleep cycles of REM and non-REM sleep per night.

Five cycles cover roughly seven hours, so make sure you're getting those hours in without hedging your bets. You need that sleep to learn. Start with seven hours. If you feel that's what you need, you're good. If not, tack on a half-hour and see how you feel. But remember, every 30 minutes you add means an even earlier bedtime. You can't hedge on the rising time!

QUALITY NOT QUANTITY

Quality sleep is what you're after.

As a modern sleeper, to obtain quality sleep, you need to set the scene to achieve it. The world is full of reasons that make it difficult to get to sleep and stay asleep, so it's incumbent on us to make the place we sleep fit for the purpose by eliminating opportunities for distractions, noise, and light pollution.

If you're having trouble getting the quality sleep you need, and that factor is a roadblock to your rising at 5 a.m. plan, it's time to get it out of the way. I'm going to tell you a bit about getting that done here, but if this problem has lasted for more than a few weeks, talk to your doctor. Sleep disorders may require medical solutions.

Here's a list of the ten most common reasons people suffer from poor sleep quality. How many of these apply to your situation?

- Eating after 8 p.m. is not good for you. Snacks are not necessary if you eat well, so if you're eating after 8 p.m, it's a habit you need to break. This could cause indigestion and trips to the bathroom that interrupt your sleep.
- The roiling brain is a problem for many who can't fall asleep. You start worrying, and then you lay there, staring at the ceiling. Change the channel. Pick up a book and read – but not in your room. Your bed is for sleep.
- The room temperature may also be throwing you off course, so check your thermostat.

- Too hot? Too cold? Remember that a cooler room generally is more suitable for sleep.
- Blue light from electronics impedes quality sleep. Keep your laptop, tablet, and mobile device out of the bedroom. After you wake up tired after your required hours of sleep, put electronics away an hour or two before bed. Blue light interferes with getting to sleep.
- Electric light is another problem. Leaving on a light in the hall can keep you awake or interrupt sleep. Turn off the lights. Sleep through the night.
- We do like our booze. But alcohol is one of the things that can interrupt your sleep cycle. It interrupts REM sleep and causes waking up in the middle of the night.

While it's a depressant, when its effects wear off, you're often undesirably wide awake. Perhaps limit your alcohol intake to the one night you're free to sleep in.

- Caffeine is another roadblock to quality sleep for some people. This stimulant is contained in coffee, energy drinks, tea, cola, cocoa, and other food products. I recommend that people pursuing 5 a.m. a lifestyle limit their caffeine intake to the morning or early afternoon. The latest you should be drinking caffeinated beverages is 2 p.m., and yes, that includes sodas containing caffeine.

- Stick to your schedule. If you're re-jigging your sleep schedule, sticking to it is the only way your body can adjust so that it will become a habit. It only takes three weeks for that to happen for most people.
- Exercising too close to bedtime elevates your heart rate and may make you restless and sleepless elusive. Rising at 5 a.m. builds in exercise time, and never strenuously exert yourself more than 2 or 3 hours before your sleep time.
- Sleep apnea is a problem for many people, obstructing breathing. Folks who live with this disorder may wake up abruptly, repeatedly throughout the night to restart breathing or wake up unrested due to reduced blood oxygen levels. You can solve this problem with medical support.

If you recognize anything on this list as a problem for you, it's time to start taking action on it. Whichever roadblock to sleep exists in your life, the only way you will successfully start rising at 5 a.m. is by addressing them.

I'm not a doctor, and I am not qualified to dispense advice on sleep disorders. But if you have a persistent problem falling asleep at night, seeing your doctor about it is crucial. In the meantime, set the stage for a good night's sleep by ensuring you're doing everything in your power to ensure that you get the sleep you need.

Some people find that a hot bath or shower before bed is helpful. If that works for you, do it. To block outside light:

- Line your curtains or put up blackout curtains.
- Use your bed only for sleep.
- Banish electronics from your sleep area.

These are some of the most important ways you can improve the quality of your sleep.

I'd recommend against pharmaceutical sleep aids. These can be habit-forming. Melatonin is likely safe, even for a few months if needed, but it can cause side effects such as headaches, irritability, stomach cramps, and dizziness. Tablets or capsules in as little as 1 mg or as great as 10 mg are available. Use the lowest dose that works for you.

Training yourself to fall asleep earlier is a project that will take some time. Your best ally in achieving your new earlier sleep time is consistency.

Go to sleep at the same time each day.

Rise at the same time each day. Even on your free day, it's a good idea not too far from usual retiring and rising times.

But reward yourself with that one sweet morning of sleeping in a little longer, as a weekly short-term reward.

A SLEEP TRICK

The United States Navy Pre-Flight School trains its pilots to fall asleep in 120 seconds. Military pilots need to be focused, alert, and ready for anything.

If that sounds like how you'd like to face the morning, read on.

Like most tricks involved in falling asleep more readily, this technique is done in stages. In the USA Navy PFS case, most pilots in the program took about six weeks to learn the technique. Once mastered, you should be able to do it whenever you need to!

Here are the steps to accomplish it:

1. Start by relaxing your face. Include the muscles inside your mouth. Many of us hold tension in our faces—especially in our mouths. Here's how you do it:

- Start by opening your mouth as widely as you can. At the same time, crinkle your nose, furrow your brow, and scrunch your eyes so that they are closed tightly. Hold this for 10 seconds, then relax. Do this three times.
- Stretch your jaw by opening your mouth slightly and then gently pushing your lower jaw forward. Hold it for 10 seconds, then relax. Now gently push your jaw to the right side so that you have an exaggerated crooked underbite. Hold it for 10 seconds, then relax. Do this three times. Repeat this for the left side.
- Blow your cheeks out as though you are playing a trumpet. Hold this pose, filling your entire mouth with air and pressure for 10 seconds. Do this three times. Now suck your cheeks inwards while holding your lips together for 10 seconds. Do three rounds of this as well.

2. Relax your shoulders and arms, then your hands. Don't move on until the muscles you're focusing on have cooperated and are relaxed. Below are 14 stretches you can do to relax your shoulders:

a. Shoulder Raises:

1. While standing or sitting with your arms by your side and with a straight back, gradually lift your shoulders in the direction of your ears.
2. Pause there here for 10 seconds.
3. Gradually lower your shoulders back down.
4. Repeat this four times.

b. Shoulder Rolls:

1. Stand or sit in an upright posture.
2. Proceed to rolling your shoulders up, back, and down.
3. Do these circles 10 times.
4. Lastly, do the reverse by rolling your shoulders up, forward, and down 10 times.

c. Ear to shoulder:

1. While sitting with a straight spine, bend your head toward your right shoulder.
2. Push as far as you can without lifting your left shoulder.

3. Intensify the stretch by using your right hand to pull your head down gently.
4. Freeze for 30 seconds.
5. Replicate on the left side.

d. Chin Retraction:

1. While standing or sitting, keep your head, neck, and spine well-aligned.
2. Reach your chin in front of you as far as it will go without struggling.
3. Next, pull your chin back into your throat and neck.
4. Do this 10 times.

e. Cross arm Stretch

1. Bring your left arm across the front of your body at about chest height.
2. Support your left arm with the elbow crease of your right arm, or use your right hand to hold your left arm.
3. Stretch out your shoulder and continue to face forward.
4. Hold this stretch for 30 seconds.
5. Repeat on the opposite side.

f. Standing arm Swings

1. While standing, place your arms by your side and open your palms to face your body.
2. Move on to swinging your arms forward, raising them as high up as they will possibly go without raising your shoulders.
3. Follow it by lowering your arms back down, bringing them as far back as you possibly can.
4. Make sure you are keeping the rest of your body very still.
5. Perform this movement for 60 seconds.

g. Standing arm lifts

1. Begin by making fists with your hands, followed by bringing them in front of your hips.
2. Move on to inhaling as you lift your arms overhead, such that your hands come together above your head.
3. Slowly lower them down back in front of your hips.
4. Perform this 10 times.

h. wide-legged standing forward bend.

1. Begin by standing with your feet wider than hip

distance, making sure your toes are pointing forward.

2. Interlock your fingers behind your back and open your chest.
3. Involve your leg muscles, making sure your knees don't bend.
4. Then pivot at the hips to bow, bringing your arms over your head in the direction of the floor.
5. Let your head hang down, tucking your chin in slightly towards your chest.
6. Stay Put in this pose for 60 seconds.

i. Cat cow pose

1. Kneel with your calves straight and toes pointing to the floor, then form a bridge with your back by placing your palms on the floor.
2. Your arms should be straight, forming a ninety-degree angle with your chest.
3. As you inhale, fill your belly with air and let it sink down as you look up.
4. Exhale as you involve your abdominals, tucking your chin into your chest, and rounding your spine.
5. Do this for two minutes.

j. Thread the needle

1. Kneel with your calves straight and toes pointing to the floor, then form a bridge with your back by placing your palms on the floor.
2. Your arms should be straight, forming a ninety-degree angle with your chest.
3. Raise your right hand and gently bring it to the left behind the left fixed on the floor. Your right palm should be facing up.
4. Rest your body on your right shoulder while turning your head to face the left.
5. Also, ensure you are not sinking onto your shoulder.
6. Hang on to this pose for half a minute.
7. Leisurely release and come back to the cat-cow pose.
8. Do the same on the opposite side.

k. Cow face pose

1. From a seated position, raise your left elbow to the side of your head with your hand facing down your spine.
2. Using your right hand, bring in your left elbow over to the right as your hand stretches further down your spine.

3. Hold the pose for 60 seconds.

4. Do the same on the opposite side.

5. Take a deep breath, then exhale it slowly and deliberately as you relax your chest and mid-section. The good news is, by performing the cat-cow pose described earlier, you were already relaxing your chest and mid-section. Double down on it by doing these other exercises:

l. Elbow Stretch

1. While standing tall, with your legs hip-distance apart, interlock your fingers behind your head, with your elbows pointing out to the sides. Gently rotate your shoulder blades back by pushing your elbows out and back, with your chest pressing forward. Hold for 20 to 30 seconds while breathing.

2. Release, be still for about 10 seconds, then repeat two to three times more.

m. Behind the Back Stretch

1. While standing tall, with your legs hip-distance apart, interlock your hands behind your back, straightening your arms.

2. Thrust your hands down to the ground, softly pressing your shoulder blades together. Be sure to shove your chest forward. Hold for 20 to 30 seconds. Relax, wait for 10 seconds, then do it again two to three more times.

A different way of going about it is to reach your arms back until each hand gets a hold of the opposite elbow. Now move on to pushing the chest out, bringing your shoulder blades altogether. This second option can be done sitting, kneeling, or standing.

n. Camel pose

While sitting on your knees, with a gap of about two fists between your knees, place your hands on your lower back, with your fingers pointing down. Twitch your belly in, lift through your chest, and bend back. Make sure your tailbone stays directed down—this is to protect your lower back. Look up at the ceiling, making sure to keep your neck long and extended. Hold for five breaths. To come out of this pose, make sure to lead with the chest forward. You can now do a child-pose or a cat-cow stretch as a counter position.

3. Now, move down to your legs. Relax the thighs, then the lower legs, then the feet. Allow them to feel floppy, like a rag doll.

Here's how:

> **a.** Sit on the ground with your legs stretched out straight in front of you; keep your toes pointed toward the ceiling.
>
> **b.** Slowly bend forward and stretch your arms toward your toes. Continue bending forward until you feel your hamstrings and calves begin to stretch. If you can, grasp your feet and hold that stretch for 10 seconds. Repeat this movement 5 times.

If you can't reach your toes yet, that is okay! Simply reach as far as you can and hold the stretch for 10 seconds. Over time, you'll notice that you're able to stretch further and further.

Never stretch to the point of pain. You should feel the tension in your muscles as they begin to release but stop the stretch immediately if you ever feel a sharp pain.

4. Clear your mind by visualizing imagery that you find relaxing for 10 seconds. I always find imagining myself sitting alone at a beach and looking as far into the sea as possible very relaxing.

5. In 10 seconds, you should be asleep.

As I said a minute ago, recruits in the PFS needed six weeks to master this valuable technique, so if you think it's for you, give it a go and stick to it until you can fall asleep effortlessly. Remember to be patient with yourself.

At the heart of techniques like these are breathing and muscle relaxation, which is validated by science as two of the conditions necessary to fall asleep. But it may not work for people who have challenges like ADHD (Attention Deficit Hyperactivity Disorder). ADHD folks tell me that a cup of coffee relaxes them, and I believe them. I've seen them fall asleep after a cup of coffee, taken in the evening. If that's you, try it. You may find it helps. This, of course, is now an exception to the no-caffeine rule.

FOR "I'M NOT A MORNING PERSON," PEOPLE

Some of you reading are undoubtedly having a tough time with the idea of rising at 5 a.m. That describes a lot of people, so don't feel bad. But you're reading because you want to change that.

You may not know this, but we all have a preferred sleep schedule. We train ourselves to adhere to this pattern. But it can be removed from your hard drive and replaced by early rising.

The first rule for becoming that shiny morning person you want to be is maintaining 9 hours of sleep, written in stone. If you need 7.5 or 8, okay, just do it consistently, and adjust your bedtime accordingly.

Before bedtime, include in your plan an hour of preparation. Have a routine that serves your morning priorities. For example, choose and lay out your clothes and perform your hygiene rituals. Pack your lunch. By going through a series of ritual actions, you will be signaling to yourself that bedtime is approaching. This serves as a cue that you're winding down for the day. That's why humans are so fond of rituals. They work!

Something you can add to your preparation ritual, right at the end, is stretching. As I've noted above, breathing and muscle relaxation are crucial for preparing your body for its nightly rest.

Stretching promotes relaxation and incorporates breathing, so programming in 10 or 15 minutes of this right before bed is something else you can do to accustom yourself to the new normal.

Before you start preparing your nighttime ritual, give your body a minute to tell you how it's feeling. You'll likely feel some tightness somewhere in your body. You may be young, my friends, but you also live with mobile devices stuck to your hands. Your neck may hurt from looking down at it for hours and absorbing the stresses of the world that day. Maybe you're on the rugby team, and you're sore all over. The act of stretching before you wind down is another way to prime your body for sleep.

NIGHT OWL NO MORE

You're ready to close your personal "night owl" chapter. You want to rise at 5 a.m. because you know it's how you'll live out your goals and life's purpose.

There's nothing wrong with being a night owl. It's what some people choose to be. Sometimes, they're night owls because of the kind of work they do.

But you're in college. College doesn't work that way if you're focused on success.

And none of this should be framed as a sacrifice. This is something much more profoundly beneficial to you. This is a re-tool of your life. Re-engineering the way you approach your life isn't about "sacrifice." It's about building the foundation of success with tools that assure the soundness of the life you're building.

This is about you and the long-term quality and success of your life. You don't have to do it. But I wrote this book because rising early can give you the edge that brings satisfaction in college, work, and fulfillment of purpose.

As you take up the behaviors I've described in this book, you'll find that rising at 5 a.m. becomes like breathing.

So, what if no one else you know is doing it? No one else is you, and no one else has decided to do what you've decided to do. With determination and self-discipline that springs from the repeated effort, you'll be revisioning yourself as a more powerful, alert, and healthy individual. It doesn't seem like a sacrifice at all when you think about it that way.

You're young, and you're smart. You've got a vision you know you must bring to fruition. I leave you with great hope for your future with this formula for a purpose-driven life marked by achievement.

CONCLUSION

It's been my profound pleasure to share all the information in this book with you. I hope you've enjoyed learning about the rising at 5 a.m. lifestyle and feeling ready to get started.

Life is to be lived with intention.

It tends to wash over us when it's not, and we never take responsibility for its quality.

But you, young reader, have already decided that option isn't for you. You want something more substantial, more exciting, and more deliberately achieved. That's why you've read this far. You're freeing yourself with an intentional approach to life that starts with a 5 a.m. alarm.

Building it is a long-term project.

It takes time, effort, and focus.

Your morning routine is your daily reminder that every day you live is a piece of your puzzle as a growing individual.

Every 5 a.m. alarm is an opportunity to work at who and what you want to be.

You've chosen a road less traveled.

With a clear vision, you're now prepared to go to bed earlier to get up earlier. With a structured plan, you're defining your goals and crafting the fullness of your life's purpose.

Supported by a new dedication to being the best you can be, you're ready to get started. And as you go forward in your journey, you're developing the habits of celebrated leaders because you want to be just like them.

This is a noble path you've begun.

Honor it by giving it everything you've got. Each day will be a sustained adventure, and you're the hero of that adventure, and you're the protagonist.

Use the tools you've discovered here to gird yourself for the life you're earning by intentionally taking responsibility for the way you live it.

I believe in action. To bring it all together, do the following now if it's not 10 p.m. yet, then return to finish reading the book:

- Pick up your alarm clock and set it for 5 a.m. tomorrow to start practicing.
- If you haven't yet, use this book as a guide to help you figure out your purpose and your goals. Your brain should have gone to work on its own already, and you will come up with ideas. Remember, these ideas will evolve, so you don't have to get stuck at this stage of the process.
- If you already knew what your purpose and goals were before reading this book, or at least had an idea, go ahead and write them down in a diary. You should have it with you all the time to ease entering ideas as they come to mind. A piece of paper that can easily go missing. Abound book is less likely to. Now pull out the daily planner of your choice (I use google calendar) and enter the following information:

5:00 a.m.- VAT (**V**isualize, **A**ffirm, and give **thanks** in advance).

5:12 a.m.- Mindfully Meditate

5:42 a.m.- Exercise

6:00 a.m.- Work on your goals

6:36 a.m.- Review purpose/goals, then plan your day out.

7:00 am-Freshen up and off to class you go (or whatever the activity will be that day).

So there. Thank you for having taken the time to read this humble offering to your future success. I would greatly appreciate your leaving a review on Amazon if you have a moment!

5 a.m. comes early, but that's no big deal when you're driven by purpose and sustained by vision. And with that thought, my friend, I wish you a future of achievement and a life of rising at 5 a.m. satisfaction! You can do this!